The New Novello Choral Edition
NOVELLO HANDEL EDITION
General Editor   Donald Burrows

Judas Maccabaeus

An Oratorio for soprano, alto (or 2 altos), tenor and bass soli,
SATB chorus and orchestra

Words by Thomas Morell

Edited by Merlin Channon

Vocal Score

Novello London

Order No: NOV 072486

Music setting by Engima

© Copyright 1998 Novello & Company Ltd.
Published in Great Britain by Novello Publishing Limited

Head Office:
14-15 Berners Street, London W1T 3LJ
Tel 020 7612 7400
Fax 020 7612 7546

Web: http://www.musicsales.com
 e-mail: music@musicsales.co.uk

Sales and Hire:
Music Sales Distribution Centre
Newmarket Road,
Bury St Edmunds,
Suffolk IP33 3YB
Tel 01284 702600
Fax 01284 768301

CONTENTS

HANDEL'S 1750 VERSION

(Movements marked * have alternative settings in Appendix One)

PART ONE

PART TWO

APPENDIX THREE
MUSIC FOR THE 1758-9 VERSION
(See p.vii for the scheme of movements for this version)

THE PERFORMING VERSIONS

The 1750 Version

From 1747 until 1759 Handel constantly varied the content of *Judas Maccabaeus*; there is, therefore, no such thing as a definitive version of the oratorio. The main text of this edition gives *Judas Maccabaeus* as presented by Handel during his 1750 London Oratorio Season. This was an expanded form of the work first performed in 1747: it included 'See, the conqu'ring hero comes' originally written for *Joshua* in 1748 and incorporated into *Judas Maccabaeus* in 1750.

Appendix One provides variant movements used in later performances during the 1750 season. It also includes No. 63b, Handel's original setting of Morell's text, 'O lovely Peace' for a solo voice. This, and the subsequent duet version, was copied into the conducting score, but only the duet version was sung at the first performance. The word-books kept to the designation 'Air' for this movement, but the conducting score provides no evidence that that version was ever used in performance during Handel's lifetime. However, from a note written in the composer's hand in the autograph score ('qui commincia il Duetto in vece dell'aria ad libitum') it appears that Handel considered the air and duet to be viable alternatives.

For the 1750 revival Handel had five soloists; a soprano, two singers for the alto-range part (a mezzo-soprano and the castrato Gaetano Guadagni), a tenor and a bass. However, the 1750 version may be performed with four soloists, with one singer for the alto/mezzo soprano part. If two singers are available, the 'alto' should sing Nos. 26, 31, 32, 35, 38, 46, 47, 52, 53 and 54, as indicated by Guadagni's name written against these movements in Handel's conducting score. Nos. 3, 4, 17, 18, 21, 24 (or 24b), 25 (or 25b), 29, 30, 48, 49, 55 and 63 could then be allocated to the mezzo-soprano.

The Original Version of 1747

There were four vocal soloists for Handel's original 1747 performances. Elisabetta de Gambarini (soprano) sang the part of the Israelitish Woman, and Caterina Galli (alto/mezzo-soprano) those of the Israelitish Man, Priest and Messenger. John Beard (tenor) sang the role of Judas Maccabaeus, and Henry Theodore Reinhold (bass) those of Simon and Eupolemus.

Appendix Two gives the variant music for the 1747 version where this differs from that in the main (1750) text. For the 1747 version, with four soloists, the following movements should be performed:

Part One   Nos. 1-5, 6b, 7-14, 16, 16b, 17-23, 27.
Part Two   Nos. 28-30, 33-47.
Part Three   Nos. 48-51, 52b, 54b, 57-64

The 1758-9 Version

Appendix Three gives the alternative scheme for the performances of *Judas Maccabaeus* during the 1758 and 1759 seasons. These were the last performances under the composer's nominal direction, although ill-health from 1752 onwards caused Handel to rely more and more on his assistant, J. C. Smith the younger. For this version the following movements should be performed:

Part One   Nos. 1-23, 24b, 25c, 26-27
Part Two   Nos. 28-30, 30b, 31-37, 37b, 37c, 38-46, 46b, 47.
Part Three   Nos. 48-51 and 52b, 54c, 55-62, 63 (or 63b), 64.

After 1750 Handel usually employed five soloists in his performances of *Judas Maccabaeus*. In 1758 the soloists were Giulia Frasi (soprano), Isabella Young (Mrs Scott) and Cassandra Frederick (alto/mezzo sopranos), John Beard (tenor) and Samuel Champness (bass). In 1759 it is possible that Giuseppe Ricciarelli replaced Cassandra Frederick.

There is scant evidence anywhere concerning the allocation of the mezzo/alto solo parts to movements for the 1758-9 performances. It is known that Handel composed items for his new singer, Frederick[1]. Walsh published Nos. 25c and 37c, 'Far brighter than the morning' and 'Great in wisdom' in 1759, with her name ascribed to them. Presumably she also sang the preceding recitatives Nos. 24b and 37b. Performance circumstances will have to be taken into consideration in allocating the movements to be sung by the two alto/mezzo-soprano soloists when reconstructing the 1758-9 version.

---

1 From a letter written by Lord Shaftesbury; see Betty Matthews, 'Handel - More Unpublished Letters', *Music and Letters* XVII (1961), pp. 127-131.

Approximate Duration:

     1750 (main-text) version: 130 minutes
        (Part One, 50 minutes; Part Two, 45 minutes; Part Three, 35 minutes)
     1758-59 version: 155 minutes
        (Part One, 50 minutes; Part Two, 65 minutes; Part Three, 40 minutes)
     1747 version: 120 minutes
        (Part One, 45 minutes; Part Two, 45 minutes; Part Three, 30 minutes)

Handel's timing in the autograph score was 105 minutes: Act One, 40 minutes; Act Two, 40 minutes; Act Three, 25 minutes.

Instrumentation:

2 Flutes, 2 Oboes, Bassoons (1 or 2), 2 Horns, 3 Trumpets, Timpani, Side Drum, Strings, Continuo (Harpsichord and Organ)

Horns and Side Drum are not required for the 1747 version.

Full score and instrumental material, including fully-realised keyboard parts, are available on hire from the publishers.

PREFACE

With a libretto supplied by Thomas Morell (1703-1784) and dedicated to William, Duke of Cumberland, Handel's *Judas Maccabaeus* was first performed at the Theatre Royal, Covent Garden on 1 April 1747, as part of his annual Lenten season of oratorios. It was well received, partly because the theme of a victorious leader was seen as having some contemporary relevance, following the suppression of the Jacobite rebellion by the Duke of Cumberland and his army at Culloden on Wednesday, 16 April 1746.

In the autograph score, Handel noted that he began *Judas Maccabaeus* on the 8th or 9th July 1746. But there is evidence that the composer had received the libretto considerably earlier. The original printed word-book of *Judas Maccabaeus* has a footnote to the air 'Come ever-smiling Liberty', stating that the text of the air 'O Liberty' was 'design'd, and wrote, for this Place, but it got, I know not how, into the *Occasional Oratorio*, and was there incomparably Set, and as finely executed'. The *Occasional Oratorio* was first performed on 14 February 1746: this suggests that Handel had read the libretto of *Judas Maccabaeus* either at the end of 1745 or by the beginning of 1746, when the Jacobite invasion was a serious threat to the peace and prosperity of the nation. At that time it would have been premature to have celebrated the Duke's victory. Instead, Handel set the libretto aside and put together the *Occasional Oratorio*, a work designed to encourage the Hanoverian cause. Following the Culloden victory, the time for Handel to complete *Judas Maccabaeus* had come; but it was not until a year later that it received its first performance.

Morell derived the narrative of his libretto from I Maccabees 1-8 and II Maccabees 5-15 in the Apocrypha. He also used additional material from Book 12 of Flavius Josephus's *The Antiquities of the Jews*: an English translation of *The Works of Josephus* by William Whiston (1667-1752) had been published in 1736.

In the autograph score Handel noted that he had completed Part One of *Judas Maccabaeus* by 22 July 1746, Part Two by 2 August, and Part Three by 11 August. Further revisions were made by the composer before the first performance and for his later performances between 1747 and 1759, all given at Covent Garden Theatre. Handel frequently changed the oratorio by including popular music from his own works and deleting movements that he had previously added. By the time of Handel's death in 1759 *Judas Maccabaeus* had become the composer's second most popular oratorio. It received thirty-three London performances under the composer's supervision: *Messiah* had thirty-six.

SOURCES

i) PRINCIPAL MANUSCRIPT SOURCES

A London, British Library RM 20.e.12. Handel's draft composition score now including the music for Nos. 1-14, 16-23, 27-30, 33-52b, 54b and 57-64. Handel used 'Act', not 'Part' to describe each of the three main sections. In this score Handel made many revisions during the process of composition, especially to Nos. 1, 17, 27, 63 and 64.

B Hamburg, Staats-und Universitätsbibliothek Carl von Ossietsky, MA/1026 (3 vols.). Handel's performance score. It was originally copied from the autograph score in 1747 by J. C. Smith the elder (hereafter referred to as 'Smith') and, presumably, was the source for the original performing parts. It became Handel's working score, into which insertions were made for successive revivals. Throughout the score Smith used the word 'Part', not 'Act', to describe each of the three main sections of the work. Part One originally consisted of Nos. 1-14, 16-23 and 27: later additions were Nos. 6 and 14 (both with revised endings), 15 and 23. Part Two originally consisted of Nos. 28-30, 33-48: later additions were Nos. 30b, 31, 32, 46 and 46b. Part Three originally consisted of Nos. 48-64: later additions were the air, 'Pow'rful guardians', originally composed for *Alexander Balus*, used in the 1748 and 1756-7 revivals of *Judas Maccabaeus*, and Nos. 55, 56 and 64.

C Manuscripts and Sketches, Cambridge, Fitzwilliam Museum.
i   MU.MS.259, pp. 53 and 54: No. 15
ii MU.MS.260, p. 26: No. 56 scored for oboes, horns and bassoon
iii MU.MS.263, p. 77: No. 56 part for second horn in G written by J. C. Smith the younger.
iv MU.MS.265, pp.105-108 have part of a soprano air in the hand of J. C. Smith the younger, setting the words:
> *Future times record thy story*
> *And with wonder sing thy name:*
> *Great in wisdom, great in glory,*
> *Thee all nations shall proclaim:*

These words were used as a basis for No. 37c,

'Great in wisdom', one of the insertions found in the printed word-book of 1758, with the couplets reversed.

ii) LIBRETTO SOURCES

L1 Huntington Library, San Marino, California, U.S.A. Larpent Collection, LA 65. Manuscript libretto in the hand of Smith and signed by the composer. It was submitted to the Inspector of Stage Plays shortly before the first performance in 1747.

L2 Printed word-book, *JUDAS MACCHABAEUS. A SACRED DRAMA. As it is Performed at the THEATRE-ROYAL in COVENT-GARDEN.* Printed for J. Watts and sold by B. Dod and dated 1747. Exemplars are British Library, CUP 407. KK.2, and Bibliothèque Nationale, Paris, Schoelcher Collection, V.S. 892. This was also re-issued for revivals of the oratorio, but with alterations to correct previous printing erors, or addenda slips indicating changes made by Handel to the oratorio. A further seven issues (with small variations) were produced between 1747 and 1750.

L3 Royal College of Music, XX.G22, vol. 11 (10). One of the later issues of Watts and Dod word-book, dated 1747. An inserted slip relates to revisions dating from 1750. Its content, as amended, is identical with **L4**, except that the text of No.25, 'May balmy peace' is pasted over No. 25b, 'Endless fame', suggesting that this change was made for the later 1750 performances.

L4 Gerald Coke Handel Collection, C4. 2nd edition of the printed word-book, dated 1750. This new edition had a few presentational variations from its immediate predecessor, but its content was exactly the same.

L5 British Library, 11778.g.17, Rowe Library, King's College, Cambridge, Mn. 20.64, and Coke Handel Collection, C7. For the one revival in 1757 a new word-book was published by Watts and Dod, and this was used, supplied with addenda slips, for the 1758 and 1759 seasons. All the exemplars have these addenda slips attached in identical places.

iii) SECONDARY MANUSCRIPT SOURCES

The following music manuscripts, with contents derived from the primary sources, are listed in what I believe to be the chronological order of their origin. All have been examined, but only copies **D**, **E**, **H**, **I** and **J** contribute new material for this edition.

D British Library, RM 18.f.10. Full score in the hand of Smith. The original owner was probably John Stanley, whose book plate appears on the inside of the front cover. It was copied c.1747 and its contents reflect closely the 1747 performing version.

E1 Manchester Public Library, Henry Watson Music Library, Newman Flower Collection, MS 130 Hd4, v.173. This score, formerly part of the Aylesford Collection, was transcribed for the library of Charles Jennens by the copyist S2[2]. The composition dates as written by Handel in **A** were transcribed into this score. It is the only copy to include the Dead March which followed the Ouverture in **A**, but which was never performed. Copied c.1747, its contents reflect the oratorio in its early state, before Handel's final revisions for the first performance.

E2 Henry Watson Music Library, Newman Flower Collection, MS 130 Hd 4, vv. 174-186, 243-244, 247-248. A set of orchestral and vocal parts of the oratorio from the Aylesford Collection copied from **E1** by S2 for Charles Jennens.

E3 Henry Watson Music Library, Newman Flower Collection, MS 130 Hd 4, v. 300. This volume from the Aylesford Collection includes scores of both the *Concerto in the Oratorio of Judas Maccabaeus* HWV 334 (probably played before Part Three at the first performance), and *The March in Judas Maccabaeus*. Both were copied for Charles Jennens by S2.

F Wimbourne St Giles, Dorset, Collection of the Earl of Shaftesbury, reference A3. This score was copied for the fourth Earl of Shaftesbury (1711-1771) by Smith, and is preceded by a contents list in his hand. 'March' is scrawled in by another hand at the end of No. 28, 'Fall'n is the foe', but no music for it was provided: the March was performed after No. 28 in Handel's 1748 revivals. The music text in this source is that of the 1747 version.

G London, Royal College of Music Library, MS.250. Score in three volumes. Copied by S5, it dates from c.1760. S5 derived the copy from **E1**, but he copied movements No. 15, 'O Liberty' and No. 55, 'See, the conqu'ring hero comes' from other sources.

---

2   Sigla for copyists are those given by Jans Peter Larsen in Handel's 'Messiah' (London, 1957).

H Gerald Coke Handel Collection. The main part of this undated score[3] is in the hand of two unidentified scribes. The first and third parts, designated here as Acts, are in one hand; the second part is in another. The music was copied originally from a source which reflected the 1747 version, but the following later items were incorporated into the score:

No. 26 (introduced in 1750) written in by yet another hand.

No. 56 (in its 1748 position, following No. 28). At the end of Nos. 52b and 54b (the original setting of 'From Capharsalama') Smith wrote, 'See the Con:/ and March'. Inserted within this movement is a separate sheet on which is written:

Recitative ends 'desolation to the land'
Chorus of Youths ends 'Songs of triumph to him sing' Chorus of Virgins ends 'to deck the Hero's brow divine'.

Then, copied by another hand, is the bass part of the last section of No. 55, with its libretto written underneath.

I Cambridge, Fitzwilliam Museum Library, MU.MS.809. Score, copied c.1760 by S9, from a set of manuscript scores of Handel's music acquired in the nineteenth century by Henry Barrett Lennard. Among the items included in the main text is No. 15 'O Liberty', with its short ending, as performed in the 1748 revival of *Judas Maccabaeus*.[4] Other additions at the end of this score were copied c.1761-63 by Smith and S5.[5] These are No. 56 in F (as used in the Concerto in Judas Maccabaeus, HWV 334), followed by Nos. 31, 30b, 37b, 24b and 26.

J Birmingham University Library, Barber Institute, Shaw Hellier Collection, MSS.75-77, (3 vols). The score was devised by using Walsh's printed editions **W1** and **W2**, supplementing them with manuscript copies of recitatives, choruses and other music not supplied by Walsh. Movements in this score include:

Vol. 1 No. 25c, 'Far brighter than the morning' (1758 addition)

Vol. 2 No. 56, the G major March, here following No. 28 (its 1748 revival position)

No. 37c 'Great in wisdom' (1758 addition)

No. 46b 'Wise men, flatt'ring' (1758 addition)

Vol. 3 No. 52b and 54b (the original setting of 'From Capharsalama', ending in A major). Following this, the words 'Chorus of Youths etc' were written.

At the end of the score there is a seven-page supplement containing No. 55.

The score and the manuscript orchestral and vocal parts associated with it were probably used for local performances at Wombourne, Worcestershire, initiated by Sir Samuel Hellier.[6]

K British Library, RM 18.f.1. Score from the 'Smith Collection' copied by S10, and dated 1766.[7] Items in the main text include some used for the 1750 and 1758-9 revivals. It also includes the longer B flat ending for No. 15, the air 'O Liberty', as used in the *Occasional Oratorio*.

iv) PRINTED EDITIONS

W1 *JUDAS MACCHABAEUS an Oratorio set to Musick by MR. HANDEL London. Printed for I. Walsh.* This earliest printed edition was published on 1 May 1747, after Handel's sixth performance. It contains the overture, airs and duets, as well as the March (added at the end), but not the recitatives and choruses. The following movements were printed:

Nos. 1, 4, 7, 10, 13, 16, 17, 18, 23, 30, 34, 35 (part 1), 37, 39 (part 1), 41, 43 (part 1), 45, 47 (part 1), 48, 51, 59, 63, 64 (part 1), 56.

Before each air and duet Walsh printed the name of the soloist(s) associated with that movement. Soloists named were Gambarini, Galli, Beard and Reinhold. Walsh reprinted this edition in 1748, and probably in 1750, but with virtually no change to the 1747 musical content.

W2 *Handel's Songs Selected from His Oratorios. For The Harpsichord, Voice, Hoboy, or German Flute. Vols. 2 and 5. London. Printed for I. Walsh.* Published in 1759, it includes Nos. 25c, 37c and 46b which were not in **W1**; these movements were incorporated into **J** using a copy of **W2**, as explained above.

LATER PRINTED EDITIONS

In 1769, William Randall, Walsh's successor, published a full score of this oratorio including the recitatives and choruses. He made use of plates from **W1** where possible, having cleaned off the singer's names and the original pagination.

3 Harvester Press Microform Publications Ltd., catalogue no. MS 216.
4 See Merlin Channon, 'Handel's Early Performances of 'Judas Maccabaeus': Some New Evidence and Interpretations', *Music and Letters*, vol.77 no. 4, November 1996, p. 517.
5 See Donald Burrows, 'The Barrett Lennard Collection', *Handel Collections and their History* (Oxford, 1993), pp. 108, 132.
6 See Percy Young, 'The Shaw-Hellier Collection', *Handel Collections and their History* (Oxford, 1993), pp. 158-170.
7 See Donald Burrows, 'The 'Granville' and 'Smith' Collections of Handel Manuscripts', in C. Banks, A Searle and M. Turner (eds.), *Sundry Sorts of Music Books* (London, 1993), pp. 234, 240, 242.

Randall's score was the first complete edition of *Judas Maccabaeus* to be published, but it does not represent any one version as performed by the composer or by J. C. Smith the younger during the composer's lifetime. In particular:

i it contains the extended ending of No. 15, 'O Liberty', which Handel did not use in this oratorio

ii No. 31, the recitative 'Well may we hope', is wrongly placed. Until No. 32 was removed from *Judas Maccabaeus* in 1764 this recitative remained in E major, but it always followed No. 30b, never preceding it. Randall misplaced this recitative, using a version ending in D major to lead into No. 30b. No. 32 was not printed in the Randall edition.

iii nos. 52b and 54b (the original settings of the recitative 'From Capharsalama') ended in A major. In 1750 it was rewritten to end in D major to lead into No. 55. No notice was taken by Randall of this change: in his edition the recitative ends in A major and is followed by No. 55 in G major.

Later ediitons were published by Harrison and Co. (1784 and 1786), Wright (c.1785), Arnold (c.1789), Preston (c.1802), Button and Whitaker (with accompaniment for the organ or pianoforte by J. Clarke, 1809), Novello and Co. (edited, and the pianoforte accompaniment arranged by Vincent Novello, 1848), Cramer, Beale (edited by George Macfarren for the English Handel Society, 1855), Breitkopf & Härtel (edited by Friedrich Chrysander, 1866), and Novello and Co. Ltd., (edited by John E. West, 1906). All contain some of the idiosyncrasies from the Randall edition, and do not distinguish Handel's performing versions.

EDITORIAL PRACTICE

The main musical sources for this edition are **A** and **B**. The overall form of the work and details of the verbal text rely on **L3** and **L4** for the 1750 version, **L1** and **L2** for the original 1747 version, and **L5** for the 1758-9 version. Obvious errors in the transcription between **A** and **B** have been tacitly corrected, but significant disagreements from these sources are noted: those of relevance to the orchestral parts only are not recorded in the vocal score, but are noted in the full score that is part of the hire material. **A** and **B** between them provide source texts for all movements except Nos. 25, 25b, 25c, 30b (bass line only in **B**), 37b, 37c, 53 and 55 (fragment only in **B**). For these, the conducting scores of the *Occasional Oratorio, Esther, Athalia, Joshua* (Hamburg, Staats- und

Universitätsbibliothek Carl von Ossietsky, MA/1033, MC/261, MC/264, MA/1027), **W2**, **I** and **J** have been treated as the main sources. Clefs have been modernised: the original clefs were soprano (C^1) for Gambarini and Galli, tenor (C^4) for Beard, bass for Reinhold. The time signature C has been retained throughout for recitatives, but replaced by 4/4 in airs, whilst key signatures have been modernised where necessary.

Punctuation and details of the verbal text have been guided by **L1**, **L2**, **L3**, **L4** and **L5**, but some modification has been made to conform to modern practice. Conventional pause signs indicating movement endings have been removed, and replaced by 'Fine' in *da capo* or *dal segno* movements. Editorial suggestions for dynamics, tempi, additional staccato dashes (e.g. No. 2, bars 3 and 4), 'delays' to emphasize significant points in the text (e.g. No. 20, bar 10), trills etc. are shown in square brackets: the precise interpretation of trills is a matter for the performers. Editorial suggestions for rhythmic alterations are shown by small-size 'flags' above or below the stave. Editorial slurs are shown thus: ⌒. In the vocal parts Handel used slurs occasionally to clarify word-underlay: these have been removed, as not needed by modern convention, except in No. 39, bars 14, 15, 50, 55, 56, 57, 58, 76 and 80, where I have considered it appropriate to highlight Handel's intentions. The crossed slur is used when such applications are the result of more controversial editorial choice, e.g. No. 18, bars 1-2, No. 48, bars 1-7, No. 63, bars 6, 7, and 9. The full score accompanying the hire material distinguishes the status of all slurs in the orchestral parts. The *hemiola*, or cadential rhythmic re-grouping in triple time, is indicated by horizontal square brackets thus: ⌐————¬.

The keyboard accompaniment is a practical reduction of the principal activity in the orchestral parts, suitable for rehearsal accompaniment: it does not pretend to include all elements of the texture. The harmonic bass line is preserved at the correct pitch as the lowest part of the accompaniment. Editorial continuo realization is distinguished from orchestral reduction by the use of small-size notes: passages accompanied by continuo alone are thus readily recognised without further markings. Keyboard realizations have taken account of Handel's sparse continuo figuring: figures from the primary sources are not printed here but are given in the full score and in the continuo part supplied with the hire material.

SOME PRACTICAL CONSIDERATIONS

i) RECITATIVES, CONTINUO ACCOMPANIMENT AND RELATED MATTERS

Recitative cadences have been printed following Handel's notation throughout. For the realization of the continuo a simple harmonic framework is provided as a basis on which players may decorate or otherwise elaborate the realization into a more varied accompaniment. Players with limited experience in continuo accompaniment can use this more or less as it stands: experienced players will have their own ideas in any case. The practical object is to give each soloist appropriate support.

Individual performance conditions will determine whether a cello should join the keyboard instrument (normally the harpsichord) in *semplice* recitatives: the recitatives are available, if needed, in the cello part supplied with the hire material. The hire material includes a fully realized principal keyboard part, and also an editorial organ part, prepared according to the principles by which Handel seems to have used the instrument. The organ principally supported the chorus, and was not the sole accompanying instrument for *semplice* recitative.

ii) MATTERS FOR SINGERS

In recitatives some appoggiaturas are shown editorially by small-stave alternatives in places where they seem appropriate. Similar practical latitude is available to singers over the ornamentation of melodic lines in airs, in the absence of any conclusive evidence. *Da capo* and *dal segno* repeats quite clearly require some form of enhancement, in which ornamentation may play a part. Frequently, however, Handel's lines are either so intrinsically decorative or so characteristic in melodic contour that ornamentation beyond the occasional shake may not be desirable or possible. Similarly, occasions for vocal cadenzas are relatively few. A pre-requisite for a cadenza is the reduction of the orchestral accompaniment in the singer's final phrase to continuo alone. One difference between the practices of Handel's vocal soloists and those of the present time is of some musical consequence. It seems virtually certain that Handel's soloists sang through the chorus movements: indeed, the 'chorus singers' may have been primarily regarded as supporters for the soloists in these movements. Thus the integration between 'solo' openings and choral continuations in movements such as No. 57 (bars 8-21) and No. 64 (bars 47-49) was effected by a perfectly natural transition as the chorus singers came in to join the soloists.

iii) THE ORCHESTRAL ACCOMPANIMENT

In general, Handel's score is precise and specific in its requirements of orchestral scoring. In appropriate places some indication of it is shown in the vocal score by abbreviations such as Vlns., Vlas., Vc., Cb., Bassi (Vc. and Cb.), Str. (for strings); Fls., Obs., Bsns., (for woodwind); Hns., Tpts., (for brass); and Timp., Side Dr., (for percussion).

The principal area of instrumental participation (apart from the continuo) that was left to habitual practice rather than specific notation concerned the oboes and bassoons. Handel included oboes in his score for Nos. 1, 2, 5, 8, 10, 11, 19, 25c, 27, 28, 30b, 34, 35, 37c, 39, 43, 46b, 47, 55, 56, 57, 59, 61 and 64.

The situation over the bassoons is rather different. In such movements as Nos. 1 (from bar 107), 5, 8, 25c, 37c and 46b the bassoon has an independent part and merits its own stave in the full score. **E2** provides evidence that the bassoon joined the orchestral bass line in movements involving the oboes. Clearly Handel expected at least two bassoons (even when performing one melodic 'part') to be included in his performances and we may reasonably infer that, rather than remaining silent for the rest of the performance, they were expected to participate from time to time in the general orchestral bass line. Editorial suggestions for their participation are made as footnotes at the beginning of certain movements.

The editorial marking '[Senza bassi]' shows Handel's use of the tenor clef to indicate where cellos provide the lowest bass tone. '[Tutti bassi]' marks his reuse of the bass clef, implying that double basses, and possibly bassoons, should play again.

iv) FURTHER EDITORIAL MATTERS

No.4   Duet   'From this dread scene'
The rhythms of the opening and closing orchestral sections differ from the corresponding vocal parts (see bars 5-7 and 15-17). A few editorial suggestions have been made above the vocal parts to match the orchestral rhythm ♩ ♫ (see bars 29, 39 and 61). I have also suggested that Solyma might be set to ♫ ♪, as used by Handel in bar 45, but, illogically, not in bar 46 or elsewhere.

No.15   Air   'O Liberty, thou choicest treasure'
In neither **B** nor **C1** did Handel name the instrument for the accompanying bass line. The editorial suggestion of a solo cello for this is shown in brackets on p.47.

HISTORY OF THE SCORE'S DEVELOPMENT

The words and music for the original 1747 performing version are both well documented. But problems arise over certain movements in the 1750 and 1758-9 revivals which were subsequently removed from the conducting score. In some cases these movements were printed or copied into secondary manuscripts, but in the following instances it has been necessary to resort to conjecture.

The 1750 Version

No. 6 Recitative 'Not vain is all this storm of grief'
No. 7 Air 'Pious orgies'

Originally Handel intended the recitative, ending in B flat, and the following air, in E flat, to be sung by Simon (bass). During its composition he decided that the air should be sung in G major by the soprano soloist. The recitative, now ending in B minor, remained with the bass soloist, as can be seen in **B**.

From 1750 onwards the recitative was transcribed for the soloist using the soprano clef. This edition gives No. 6 in this later version: the original bass version (No. 6b) is in Appendix Two. The soprano air 'Pious Orgies' remained in G major during Handel's lifetime. After his death the air was performed in E flat with the recitative ending in B flat to lead into it, as can be deduced from annotations and written comments in **B**.

No. 24 Recitative 'O Judas, may thy just pursuits'
No. 25 Air 'May balmy peace'

L3 shows that 'May balmy peace', taken from the *Occasional Oratorio*, superseded 'Endless fame', probably for later performances in 1750. In the *Occasional Oratorio* it was written in E minor, but we have no evidence that it was used in that key in 1750 for *Judas Maccabaeus*. In **B** the first line of No. 16b was set to the words 'O Judas, may these noble views inspire' and the recitative ended in B major. In 1750, when it was placed later to precede 25b, the text was amended to 'O Judas, may thy just pursuits inspire', and the recitative was transposed to end in B flat major. In **B** the recitative still ends in B flat major, which is not surprising since later revivals reverted to using the E flat air 'Endless fame'. In the *Occasional Oratorio* 'May balmy peace' was preceded by a recitative ending in B major, set to the same text as the air. I have used the original music of No. 16b, ending in B major to lead into this E minor air, rather than transposing the air down a semitone.

No. 24b Recitative 'O Judas, may thy just pursuits'
No. 25b Air 'Endless fame'

For the recitative I have used the version found in **B** on f.68v., and at the end of **I** on p.201. The air, used in the 1732 version of *Esther*, is in its conducting score, ff.32v.-34v. For *Judas Maccabaeus*, however, the middle section of this *da capo* movement was set to different words, as can be seen on the addenda slip of **L4**. These were:

> Children's children late descending
> Israel's cause like Thee defending
> Shall thy glorious worth declare.

I have been unable to find any exemplars, either in manuscript or printed form, of Handel's setting of these words. What appears in this edition is my conjecture, based on the similarity between these later words and those used in E*sther*, which were:

> Titles, all their lustre lending
> To thy latest race descending,
> Shall thy Prince's love declare.

No. 31 Recitative 'Well may we hope'
No. 32 Air 'Flowing joys'

Two versions of Nos. 31 and 32 are in **B**, giving the air in both E major and A Major. The air was adapted from 'So much beauty' in *Esther*, where it was in E major. From the names of soloists added to the movement in **B** it would appear that the A major version was the earlier, and the E major version was prepared for a revival after 1759. Both versions were copied into the score on two staves throughout, the lower stave for the continuo part and the upper stave for the soloist: the orchestral parts would have been copied separately for the performers. The original version of Nos. 31 and 32 exists on f.18 and f.18v., but part of each has been torn out. I have derived the material for these two movements (a) by transposing the E major version into A major to provide the solo and continuo parts and (b) by referring to Handel's autograph of 'So much beauty' in *Esther*, British Library, RM 20.e.7, ff.69v. - 70v.[8]

No. 46 Recitative 'Ye worshippers of God!'
'No more in Sion'
No. 47 Duet and Chorus
'O never bow we down'

These movements were copied into **B** with the music written in the soprano clef for both the Israelitish Man and Woman soloists. In **B** alternative notes were sketched in by Handel on the Israelitish Man's stave in both movements.

W records that Beard (tenor) sang in the duet, not Galli (mezzo-soprano), but whether this was at the first performance, or at another preceding

---

8 'So much beauty' is no longer in the conducting score (Hamburg, Staats-und Universitätsbibliothek, MC/261) of *Esther*.

the publication of the edition on 1 May 1747, is uncertain. To add to the mystery, the names Judas, Galli and Guadagni are annotated above the first part of the recitative in **B**. It is likely that Guadagni sang both movements in 1750, but who sang the part of the Israelitish Man in these movements at the first performance is not known. In Nos. 46 and 47 I have given Handel's alternatives in small notes on the appropriate stave, as they appear in **B**. When using the 1747 version, a choice of tenor or mezzo-soprano soloist can be made for the role of the Israelitish Man; the use of the alternative notation is a matter for performers.

No. 49   Recitative   'See, see yon flames'
In **B** the solo part of this accompanied recitative is written in the soprano clef. Annotations above the solo stave suggest that Galli (mezzo-soprano), whose name is crossed out, and Reinhold (bass), who died in 1751, sang this movement. Clearly there was a change of soloist between 1747 and 1751, but there is no evidence to show when the change occurred. If the 1747 version is being used this movement could be sung by the bass soloist.

No. 52   Recitative   'From Capharsalama'
For the first performance in 1747 Handel composed this recitative as a single unit of 27 bars for Galli (as shown in Nos. 52b and 54b). It began in C major, following the B flat major air 'So shall the lute and harp awake' (No. 51). The recitative ended in A major and led to the D major chorus 'Sing unto God' (No. 57).

For the 1750 revivals the recitative was subdivided. After section 1, which had been adjusted to end in G minor (as in No. 52), there followed the B flat air 'All his mercies' (No. 53). Sections 2 ('Yet more) and 3 ('But lo!') continued, but with alterations to end in D major (as in no. 54) to lead into the G major chorus 'See the conqu'ring hero comes' (No. 55). Section 3 was copied out with the solo part written in the bass clef, but it was annotated 'For Guadagni'. He probably sang it after performing 'All his mercies' (No. 53). We do not know when (or if) the bass clef version was performed, but it is given in this edition as an alternative on p.191, following the alto version. The solo line of No. 52 is written in the alto clef on **B**, f.11v., but annotated with the name 'Reinhold' (bass) as well as 'Guadagni' (alto). This suggests that at some (unknown) revival the bass soloist sang this part of the recitative originally designed to be sung by the Israelitish Messenger (Galli). It was later sung by Guadagni, possibly in 1750. It might be surmised that he then sang the following air.

No. 53   Air   'All his mercies I review'
This is an adaptation of the middle section of the ternary air 'Cease thy anguish' from *Athalia*, first used in *Judas Maccabaeus* for an early revival in April 1747.[9] Since I have not found this adaptation in any of the sources, I have conjectured that the first twelve bars of the original movement in the conducting score of *Athalia* were used both as an introduction and then as the closing ritornello, with a *Fine* at bar 12, beat 1 for this version.

No. 55   Chorus   'See, the conqu'ring hero comes'
No. 56   March
Only a fragment of these movements appears in **B**. For the chorus I have used the original version on ff.97-98v. in the autograph score of *Joshua* (British Library, RM 20.e.11), f.48 of its conducting score and **J**; for the March I have relied on **C**, **J** and **E3**.

The 1758-9 Version
No. 24b Recitative   'O Judas, may thy just pursuits'
No. 25c Air   'Far brighter than the morning'
The recitative remains in **B**, suggesting that it was used in the 1758-9 revivals. The copyist of **J** incorporated the air from **W2**. My keyboard version is a reduction from that printed score.

No. 30b Duet and Chorus
'Sion now.
Tune your harps'
This movement was used in the 1757 revival of *Esther* and transferred to *Judas Maccabaeus* in 1758. Only the figured bass line now remains in **B**, ff.15-16v. I have consulted ff.74-80v. of the conducting score of *Esther*, as well as pp.183-197 in **I**.

No. 37b Recitative   'Sweet are thy words'
No. 37c Air   'Great in wisdom'
'Sweet are thy words' was added at the end of I. The D minor air, part of which appears in **C4**, pp.105-108, was published in its entirety by Walsh in **W2**.

No. 466 Air   'Wise men flatt'ring'
Introduced in 1758. (See p.xi above).

Nos. 52b, 54c Recitative 'From Capharsalama'
For the 1758-9 revivals, this recitative became one unit again. But section 2 ('Yet more') now ended in A major, whilst the ending to section 3 ('But lo!') remained in D major to accommodate No. 55.

9   See Merlin Channon, op. cit., p.509.

ACKNOWLEDGEMENTS

I would like to thank the owners and the librarians of the institutions holding the sources for their help and for the kindness I have received from them. I am grateful to Donald Burrows for his advice during the preparation of this edition and to Hywel Davies for seeing it through the press.

Merlin Channon, 1998

JUDAS MACCABAEUS

AN ORATORIO
Words by Thomas Morell (1703-1784)

DRAMATIS PERSONAE

Judas Maccabaeus, commander of the Israelite army [Tenor]
Simon, brother to Judas; religious leader of the Israelites [Bass]
Israelitish Woman [Soprano]
Israelitish Man [Mezzo-soprano or Alto]
Israelitish Priest [Mezzo-soprano or Alto]
Messenger [Mezzo-soprano or Alto]
Eupolemus, Israelite Ambassador to Rome [Bass]
Chorus of Israelites

The Historical Background

The Maccabean Revolt in the second century B.C. provided the background to the story unfolded in *Judas Maccabaeus*. It is part of the history of the Ptolemaic and Seleucid Empires.

Following the death of Alexander the Great in Babylon in 323 B.C., his empire disintegrated. When his own descendants were unable to succeed him effectively, the kingdom went to his Generals. Two of these were Ptolemy, who assumed the Kingship of Egypt, and Seleucus, who established himself first as master of Babylonia, and later of the northern part of Syria, where he made Antioch his capital.

Palestine initially remained under Ptolemy, but by 198 B.C., in the reign of Antiochus the Great, Palestine was finally conquered by the Syrians. Under Antiochus the Jews were favourably treated, but later, under his successor Antiochus IV (Antiochus Epiphanes), the Jewish people suffered great hardship. Like Alexander the Great, he sought to impose both a common Greek culture and its religion (Hellenism) on his empire. In 169 B.C. Jerusalem was attacked. In 167 B.C. Jewish religious customs were forbidden, the Temple was defiled and pagan rites were instituted.

There followed a rebellion led by Mattathias, a priest of the Joarib family from Jerusalem who had settled in Modin. It was continued by his sons John, Simon, Judas Maccabaeus, Eleazar and Jonathan after Mattathias's death in 166 B.C. Morell's libretto begins here and continues the outline of the Maccabean struggle until 161 B.C.

Having dealt with the appointment of Judas as the military leader of the nation, Morell takes the story, in a condensed form, down to 164 B.C., when Judas marched on Jerusalem and regained the Temple for the Jews; subsequently the Temple was purified and reconsecrated. Further wars were fought by the armies of Judas and his brothers during the reigns of Antiochus IV, who died in 163 B.C., and his successor, Antiochus V, but these were not recorded with historical accuracy in the libretto: Judas's victory as outlined in Part Three is a fanciful amalgam. In a footnote before the recitative 'From Capharsalama' in the original printed word-book Morell explained:

> *Several Incidents were introduced here by way of* Messenger, *and* Chorus, *in order to make the Story more compleat, but it was thought they would make the Performance too long, and therefore were not Set, and therefore not printed; this being design'd, not as a finish'd Poem, but merely as an Oratorio.*

SYNOPSIS

PART ONE

The Israelites mourn the death of Mattathias, their leader in the struggle against the persucution of Antiochus Epiphanes, King of Syria. They appeal to God to grant them another leader. Simon, one of Mattathias's sons, rallies the Israelites, telling them to put their trust in God. Claiming divine inspiration, he proclaims his brother, Judas Maccabaeus, the new commander.

Judas addresses his followers, calling on them to be inspired by the battle honours of their forefathers. The Israelites offer prayers for their newly appointed leader and for the restoration of their liberty. Judas demands that his troops face the enemy resolved on liberty or death. Part One ends with the Israelites imploring the Almighty to support them in their struggle.

PART TWO

Judas receives the acclaim of his people, having defeated one group of invaders from Samaria led by Apollonius, and another from Syria under the command of Seron. Judas acknowledges their acclaim, but tells them to give thanks to Almighty God. News then arrives that King Antiochus has decided to dispatch an army from Egypt under General Gorgias to destroy the Jewish nation. The Israelites are in despair, but Simon tries to comfort them, telling them to turn to God, since He alone can work wonders.

Declaring Jehovah his leader, Judas once again calls on his troops to fight. They declare their loyalty to him and their willingness to die for their laws, their religion and their liberty. Simon, approving of his brother's rallying call, tells him that he will be responsible for restoring the Temple recently desecrated by the Syrians. He believes that its restoration is vital if God is to give Israel success in battle. The Israelites vow not to worship heathen idols, as ordered by the Syrian king, but to worship God, and God alone.

PART THREE

Part Three opens after the Temple has been returned to the Israelites and reconsecrated. In commemoration, a Festival of Thanksgiving is to be celebrated, and since the ceremonial lighting of lamps was a prominent feature of this, it became known as the Feast of Lights.

In the next scene an Israelitish Messenger arrives bearing the news of the rout of the invaders by Judas at Capharsalama. The Israelites sing unto God 'with unmeasured praise'. Judas enters in triumph and is greeted enthusiastically by his countrymen. He asks for those killed in battle to be remembered, and especially Eleazar, his brother, who triumphed in a glorious death. He had attacked a heavily guarded armoured elephant which he assumed to be carrying the enemy's king. Getting under the elephant, he stabbed it; whereupon the elephant collapsed on top of Eleazar, killing him.

In the final scene Eupolemus, the Israelite Ambassador, returns from a mission to Rome with a treaty ensuring protection for Judea as an independent nation. With grateful hearts the Israelites pay tribute to God for the blessings they have received: they also show their gratitude to Judas Maccabaeus. The story ends with the Israelites looking forward to peace and prosperity. On Simon's orders the Israelites rejoice with the celestial spirits, Cherubim and Seraphim, singing 'songs divine'. A fine Hallelujah Chorus ends the oratorio.

This synopsis and its historical background may be freely reproduced in concert programmes. Acknowledgement should be made to Novello & Co. Ltd.

JUDAS MACCABAEUS
PART ONE
OUVERTURE

No. 1

Bars 102-103: E♭ tied in **A**, but not in **B**.

* See Preface, p. xiii.

Bar 150: marked 'Lentement' by Handel in **A**. This was omitted in **B**.

Bar 157, beats 3-4: Vln. 2 and Vla. have the rhythm ♪ 𝄽 𝅘𝅥𝅮𝅘𝅥𝅮 in **B**, but not in **A**.

No. 2   Chorus MOURN, YE AFFLICTED CHILDREN

Chorus

* See Preface, p. xiii.

8

Bar 22, beat 2: Handel's dynamic marking in **A** was not copied into **B**.
Bar 23: both chorus parts are marked '**_f_**' in **A**, but not in **B**.

10

Bar 46, beat 1: Handel's rhythm for Vln. 1 was ⌐⌐ in **A**. This was copied as ⌐.⌐ in **B**.

No. 3   Recitative WELL MAY YOUR SORROWS
Israelitish Man, Israelitish Woman

ISRAELITISH MAN

Well may your sor - rows, breth - ren, flow in all th'ex -

Cont.

- pres - sive signs of woe; your soft - er gar - ments tear, and

squa - lid sack - cloth wear; your droop - ing heads with ash - es

strew, and with the flow - ing tear your cheeks be - dew.

ISRAELITISH WOMAN

Daugh - ters, let

your dis-tress-ful cries and loud la-ment as-cend the skies. Your snow-y bo-soms beat, and tear, with hands re- -morse-less, your di-shev-ell'd hair. For pale and breath-less, Mat-ta-thi-as lies, sad em-blem of his coun-try's mi-se-ries.

(tender)

[segue]

Bar 12, beat 3: **A, B, L** have 'snowy', **L2** has 'tender'.

No. 4   Duet FROM THIS DREAD SCENE

Israelitish Man, Israelitish Woman

Bar 12: the lower option was later annotated in **B**.
Bar 15 onwards: see Preface, p. xiii, where the matter of matching the rhythms of the vocal and orchestral parts (editorially) is considered.

15

35

scene,— O So - ly - ma, — ky ru — ins lie. From this dread

[tr]

39

thy boast - ed tow'rs in smo — — — ky ru - ins
scene these ad - verse pow'rs, ah! whi - ther shall we

[tr]

43

lie. O So - ly - ma, O
fly? ah! whi - ther shall we fly? O So - ly - ma,

47

thy boast - ed— tow'rs in smo-ky ru - ins lie,
So - ly - ma, thy boast - ed— tow'rs in smo-ky ru - ins

18

No. 5   Chorus FOR SION LAMENTATION MAKE

Chorus

20

22

No. 6   Recitative NOT VAIN IS ALL THIS STORM OF GRIEF

Israelitish Woman

No. 7   Air   PIOUS ORGIES

Israelitish Woman

Bar 18, beat 1: the two quavers for strings are in **B**, but not in **W1**.

No. 8 Chorus O FATHER, WHOSE ALMIGHTY POW'R

Chorus

No. 9   Accompanied Recitative I FEEL THE DEITY WITHIN

Simon

[segue]

No. 10   Air   ARM, ARM, YE BRAVE

Simon

zeal de - mands.

Tutti

In de - fence of your na - tion, re -

-li - gion, and laws, th'Al - migh - ty Je - ho - vah will strength - en your hands.

Vlns.

In de - fence of your na - tion, re - li - gion, and laws,

th'Al - migh - ty Je - ho - vah will strength - - - - - - -

68

_____ en, th'Al - migh - ty Je - ho - vah will

72

strength - en your hands. Arm, arm,

Vlns. unis.

[f] [. .] [p]

76

arm, arm, ye brave; a no - - ble cause, the cause_____ of Heav'n de -

79

-mands your_ zeal, a no - - ble cause, arm, arm, ye brave,

Obs.

82

arm, arm, ye brave; the cause_____ of Heav'n_____ your zeal de -

[segue]

No. 11   Chorus WE COME IN BRIGHT ARRAY

Chorus

* See Preface, p. xiii.

Recitative 'TIS WELL, MY FRIENDS

Judas Maccabaeus

'Tis well, my friends; with trans-port I be-hold the spi-rit of our fa-thers, fam'd of old for their ex-ploits in war. Oh, may their fire with ac-tive cour-age you, their sons, in - spire; as when the migh-ty Josh-ua fought, and those a - maz-ing won-ders wrought; stood still, o - be-dient to his voice, the sun, 'till kings he had des - troy'd, and king-doms won.

No. 13 Air CALL FORTH THY POW'RS

Judas Maccabaeus

Bar 29, beat 1: Vln. 1 also has F♯ in **A** , but not in **B** .

No. 14   Recitative TO HEAV'N'S IMMORTAL KING WE KNEEL

Israelitish Woman

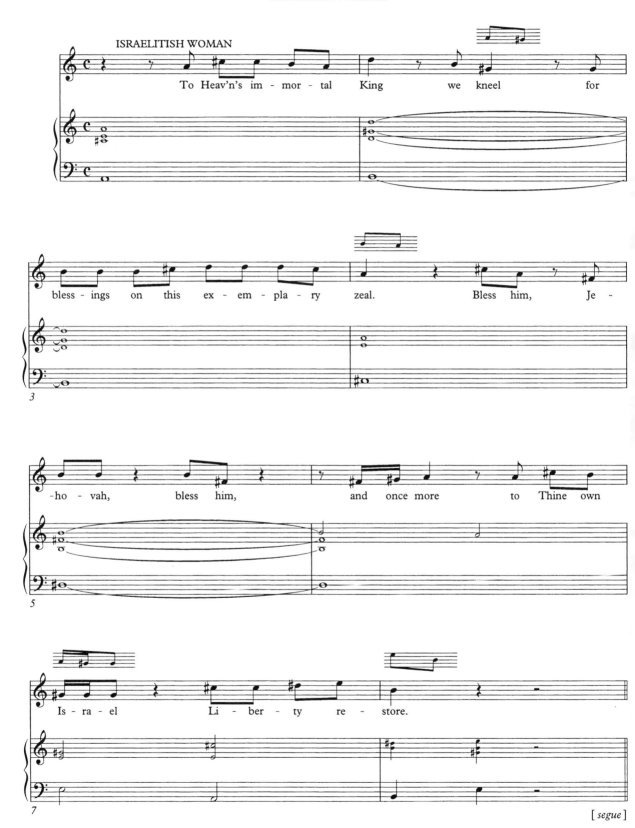

[_segue_]

Bar 1: 'immortal' in **A**, **B**, **L1**, 'almighty' in **L2**.
Bar 6: 'Thine own' in **L2-5**, 'Thy own' in **A**, **B**, **L1**.

No. 15   Air O LIBERTY, THOU CHOICEST TREASURE

Israelitish Woman

O Li - ber - ty, thou choic - est trea - sure, seat of virtue, source of plea - sure; life with - out___ thee knows no bless - ing, no en- -dear - ment worth ca - ress - ing, no en - dear - ment worth__ ca - ress - - - - - - - ing, no en - dear - ment worth ca - ress - - ing.

* See Preface, p. xiii.

No. 16   Air COME, EVER-SMILING LIBERTY

Israelitish Woman

ISRAELITISH WOMAN

Come, ev - er - smil - ing Li - ber-ty,

and with thee bring thy jo - cund train. Come, ev - er -

-smil - ing Li - ber-ty, and with thee bring thy jo - cund train. Come, ev - er-smil - ing,

Bar 22: although not in **A**, the first three quavers, shown here at the top of the continuo part, were copied into **B** and printed in **W1**.
Handel originally indicated by sign in **A** that the vocal notation should be doubled from bar 13 until bar 22, where he wrote the first three quavers of the singer's part. These instructions were not followed in **B**.
Bar 25, 3rd quaver, voice: lower alternative note is in both **A** and **B**.

jo - cund___ train, thy   jo - cund___ train,   and with thee bring   thy

jo - cund train.   For

thee_ we pant, and sigh   for thee,   we   pant   for thee,   with

whom e - ter - nal   plea - sures reign. For   thee we pant,   we   sigh   for thee,

with whom e - ter - nal   plea - sures reign.   Come,   ev - er -

-smil - ing Li - ber-ty, and with thee bring— thy jo - -cund train.

62

Come, ev - er - - - smil - ing Li - ber - ty, come, ev - er - -

66

-smil - ing Li - ber - ty, and with thee bring thy jo - cund train, thy jo - cund, jo - -

70

- cund train, and with thee bring thy

74

jo - - cund train.

78

No. 17   Air 'TIS LIBERTY

Israelitish Man

54

Bar 22, beat 4: Vlns. have crotchet B♮ in **A** and **B**.

Bar 34, beat 1: crotchet G♯ for Vlns. in **B**.

No. 18   Duet COME, EVER-SMILING LIBERTY

Israelitish Woman, Israelitish Man

No. 19   Chorus LEAD ON, LEAD ON

Chorus

3

* See Preface, p. xiii.

No. 20   Recitative SO WILL'D MY FATHER, NOW AT REST

Judas Maccabaeus

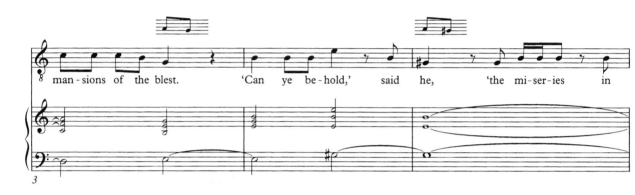

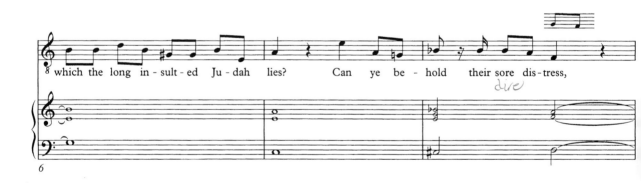

Bar 8, beats 2-3: 'sore distress' in **A**, **B**, **L1**; only **L2** has 'dire distress'.

Accompanied Recitative

In this arrangement of the string accompaniment it might be more convenient to play crotchets in the left hand, rather than the original semiquavers from bar 14.

No. 21   Semi-Chorus DISDAINFUL OF DANGER

Semi-Chorus*

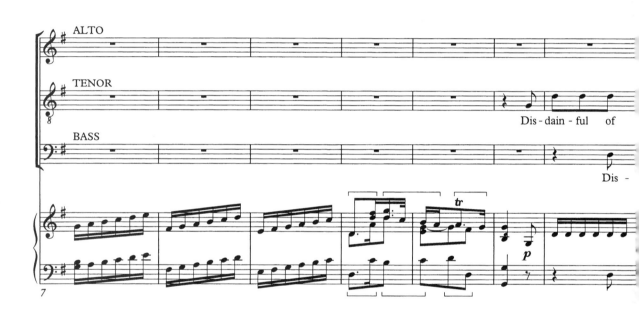

* Annotations in **B** suggests that this movement was sung by the soloists.

68

No. 22   Recitative AMBITION! IF E'ER HONOUR WAS THINE AIM

Judas Maccabaeus

No. 23   Air NO UNHALLOW'D DESIRE

Judas Maccabaeus

* Vlns. double the bass part an octave higher throughout the movement.

more,___ no more, no more, no more,___

and con-quest shall ask___ no more. But peace___ to___ ob - tain, free

peace___ let___ us gain, and con - quest shall ask___ no more.

[tr]

[f]

No. 24   Recitative   O JUDAS, MAY THY JUST PURSUITS

Israelitish Man

Bar 2: 'thy' in **B** , 'these' in **L3** , **L4** and **L5**.

No. 25   Air   MAY BALMY PEACE

Israelitish Man

whose God and peo - ple are his____ care!

Bar 71-2: the decoration of the solo part is annotated, without the trill, in the conducting score of the *Occasional Oratorio* .

No. 26   Recitative **HASTE WE, MY BRETHREN**

Israelitish Man

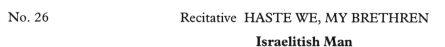

ISRAELITISH MAN

Haste we, my breth - ren, haste we to the field, de -

Cont.

-pen - dent on the Lord, our strength and shield.

No. 27   Chorus   HEAR US, O LORD

Chorus

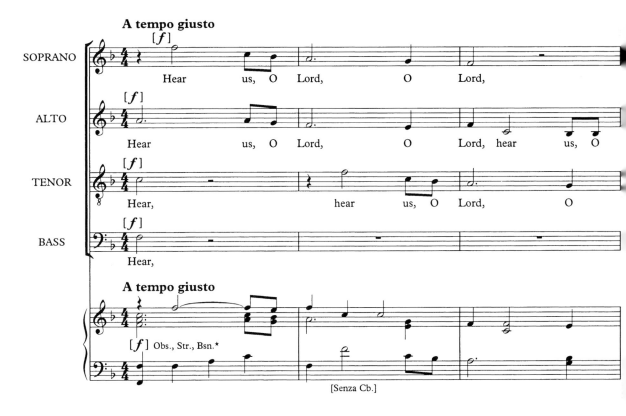

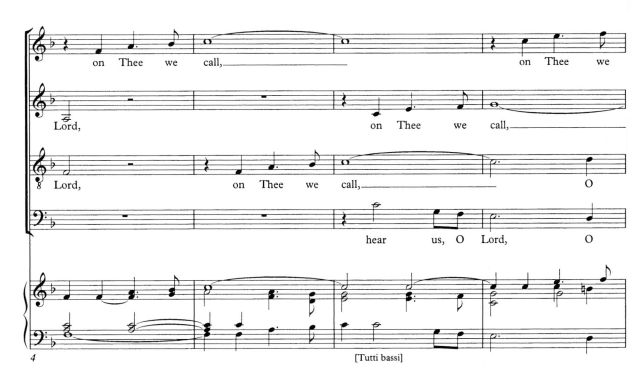

84

END OF PART ONE

PART TWO

No. 28

Chorus FALL'N IS THE FOE

Chorus

* See Preface, p. xiii.

Recitative **VICTORIOUS HERO!**

Israelitish Man

ISRAELITISH MAN

Vic- to- rious he- ro! Fame shall tell, with her last breath, how

A- pol- lo- nius fell, and all Sa- ma- ria fled, by thee pur-

-sued through hills of car- nage and a sea of blood. While

thy re- sist- less prow- ess dealt a- round, with their own lead- er's

sword, thy death- ful wound. Thus, too, the haugh- ty Se- ron, Sy- ria's

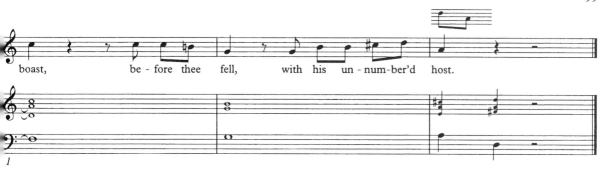

boast, be - fore thee fell, with his un - num-ber'd host.

No. 30 Air SO RAPID THY COURSE IS

Israelitish Man

Allegro

Vlns. unis.

[*f*]

100

So rap-id thy course is,— not— num-ber-less for-ces with-stand thy

ad libitum [a tempo]

all — — con - quer-ing sword.

[colla voce]

Str. *f*

FINE

Though na - tions— sur - - round thee, no pow'r shall con -

No. 31   Recitative WELL MAY WE HOPE

Israelitish Man

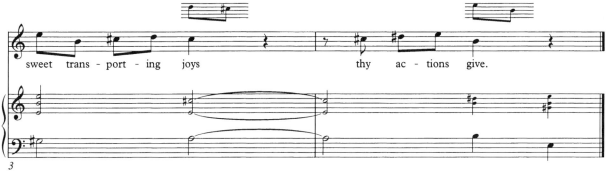

Bar 3: 'transporting joys' in **B**; 'transporting views' in **L3** .

No. 32   Air FLOWING JOYS

Israelitish Man

ISRAELITISH MAN

Flow - - ing— joys do— now sur-round me,

No. 33   Recitative O LET ETERNAL HONOURS CROWN HIS NAME

Israelitish Woman

I MACCABEES iii, 3-4

No.34   Air   FROM MIGHTY KINGS HE TOOK THE SPOIL

Israelitish Woman

* See Preface, p. xiii.
Bar 1: the trill that Handel added under the F♯ in **A** was not copied into **B**, nor was it printed in **W1**.

Ju - - dah smile, _____

and with _ his acts _____ made Ju - dah smile.

FINE

Allegro

Ju - dah re - joic - - - - - - - - eth, re - joic - eth in his

Allegro

[p]

No. 35   Duet and Chorus   HAIL, JUDEA, HAPPY LAND!
Israelitish Man, Israelitish Woman, Chorus

[segue]

118

No. 36 Recitative THANKS TO MY BRETHREN
Judas Maccabaeus

Bar 4: bass line as in **A** and **B**.
A semibreve 'a', with 'g♮' transferred to the stave above is an editorial suggestion.

No. 37   Air HOW VAIN IS MAN WHO BOASTS IN FIGHT

Judas Maccabaeus

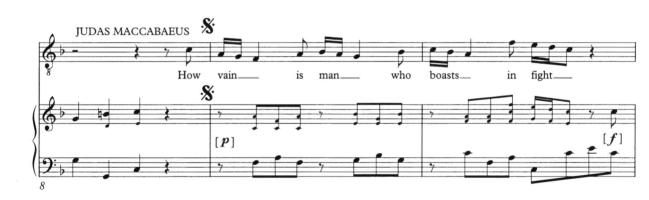

Bar 3, beat 4: Handel wrote a trill in **A**. It was not copied into **B**, but it was printed in **W1**.

Bar 40: Bass as in **A** . **B** has

126

Recitative O JUDAS, O MY BRETHREN!

Israelitish Messenger

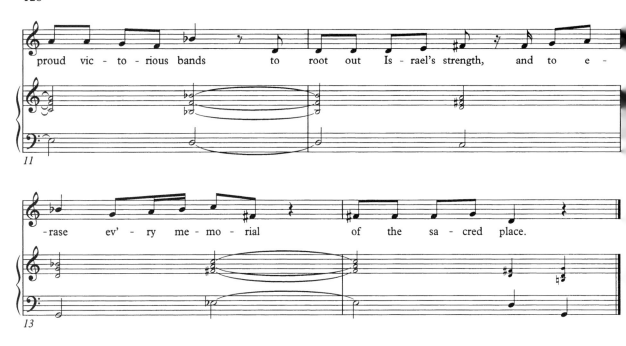

proud vic - to - rious bands to root out Is - rael's strength, and to e -

-rase ev' - ry me - mo - rial of the sa - cred place.

No. 39   Air and Chorus AH! WRETCHED ISRAEL!

Israelitish Woman, Chorus

Largo

[*p*]

Solo cello

[*tr*]

ISRAELITISH WOMAN

[*tr*]

Ah! wretch - ed,—

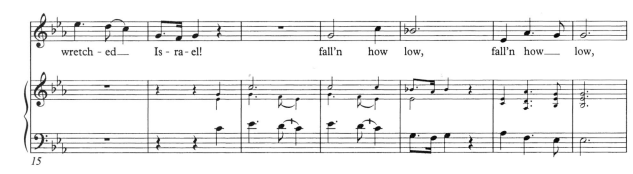

wretch - ed— Is - ra - el!   fall'n how low,   fall'n how— low,

Bar 30: 'v. pianiss°' in **B**.

joy - ous trans - port to des - pond - ing woe, fall'n how low, from joy - ous

joy - ous trans - port to des - pond - ing woe, fall'n how low, from joy - ous

joy - ous trans - port to des - pond - ing woe, fall'n how low, from joy - ous

joy - ous trans - port to des - pond - ing woe, fall'n how low, from joy - ous

114

Adagio

trans - port to des - pond - - ing, des - pond - - ing woe.

trans - port to des - pond - - ing, des - pond - - ing woe.

trans - port to des - pond - - ing, des - pond - - ing woe.

trans - port to des - pond - - ing, des - pond - - ing woe.

Adagio

121

128

No. 40   Recitative BE COMFORTED

Simon

Bar 6-7: 'demerit' in **A**, **B**, **L1**, 'demerits' in **L2** .

No. 41   Air THE LORD WORKETH WONDERS

Simon

136

Bar 20, beat 4: vocal line as in **A**, **B** and **W1**.

still— as He thun-ders, is fear - ful in praise.

No. 42   Recitative MY ARMS! AGAINST THIS GORGIAS WILL I GO

Judas Maccabaeus

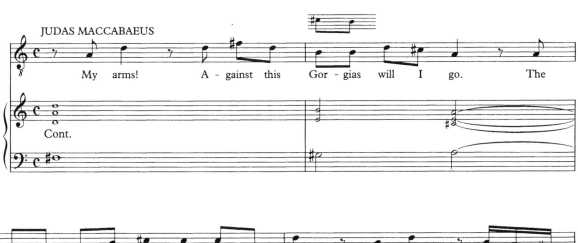

JUDAS MACCABAEUS

My arms! A - gainst this Gor - gias will I go. The

I - du - me - an Go - ver - nor shall know how vain, how in - ef -

-fec - tive his de - sign, while rage his lead - er, and Je - ho - vah mine.

[*segue*]

No. 43

Air and Chorus SOUND AN ALARM

Judas Maccabaeus, Chorus

* See Preface, p. xiii.

and call the___ brave, and___ on-ly___ brave, and on-ly brave a-

-round.   Sound an a-larm.

Your sil - ver trum-pets sound,

and call the___ brave, and___ on-ly___ brave, and on-ly brave a-

-round.

144

146

No. 44   Recitative ENOUGH! TO HEAV'N WE LEAVE THE REST

Simon

Air WITH PIOUS HEARTS

Simon

150

*Indicated thus in source **B**, but possibly
na - tions

Bars 70-71: the appoggiaturas here, corresponding with Handel's in bars 1 and 2, are editorial.

Recitative YE WORSHIPPERS OF GOD!

Israelitish Man, Israelitish Woman

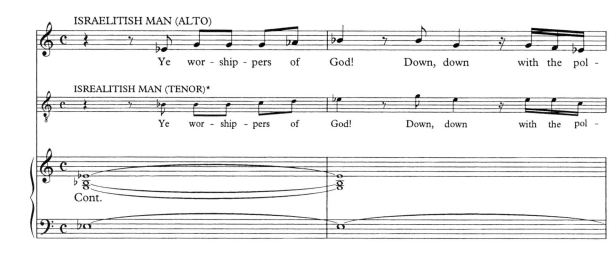

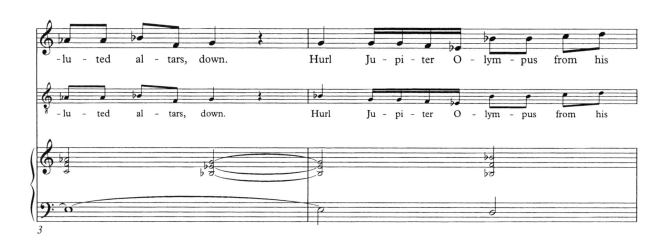

* The small-note staves give the version sung in 1747 by the Tenor who also sang the part of Judas Maccabaeus. See Preface, p. xiv.

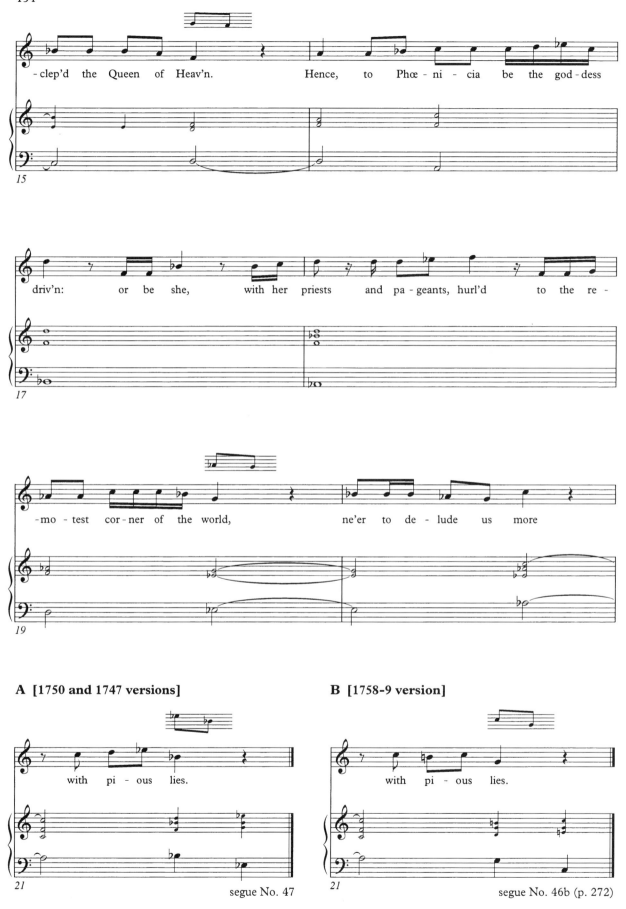

A [1750 and 1747 versions]

with pi - ous lies.

B [1758-9 version]

with pi - ous lies.

segue No. 47

segue No. 46b (p. 272)

Bars 14-15: 'yclep'd' (called) as in **L1** and **L2**. Handel misunderstood the word. In **A** he wrote 'eclips'd'. In **B** it was copied as 'yclips'd'.

No. 47   Duet and Chorus   O NEVER BOW WE DOWN

Israelitish Woman, Israelitish Man, Chorus

* The small-note staves give the version sung in 1747 by the Tenor who also sang the part of Judas Maccabaeus. See Preface, p. xiv.

Bars 34, 36-38: Handel's alternatives for the Israelitish Woman and Israelitish Man (Alto), presumably made after 1747, are shown in small notes.
See Preface, p. xiv.

stone, never, never bow we down,
stone, never, never bow we
stone, never, never bow we

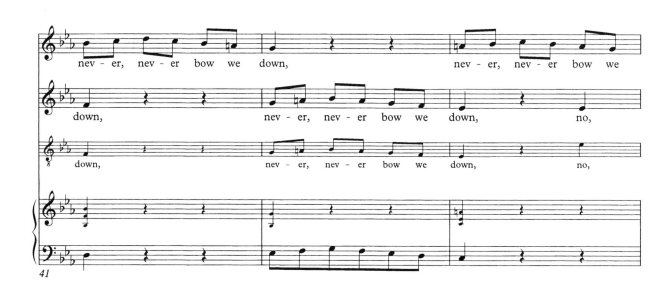

never, never bow we down, never, never bow we
down, never, never bow we down, no,
down, never, never bow we down, no,

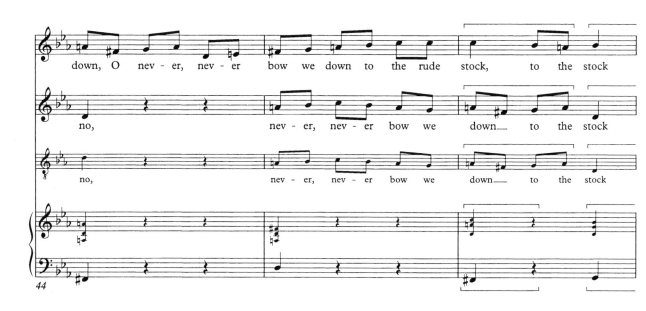

down, O never, never bow we down to the rude stock, to the stock
no, never, never bow we down to the stock
no, never, never bow we down to the stock

His aw - ful nod.

His aw - ful nod.

His aw - ful nod.

63

ISRAELITISH WOMAN

O nev - er, nev - er bow we

ISRAELITISH MAN (ALTO)

O nev - er, nev - er bow we down,

ISRAELITISH MAN (TENOR)

O nev - er, nev - er bow we down,

69

down, nev - er, nev - er bow we down, O nev - er, nev - er

nev - er, nev - er bow we down,

nev - er, nev - er bow we down, no, no,

72

bow we down to the rude stock or sculp - - tur'd

nev - er, nev - er bow we down to the rude stock or sculp - - tur'd

nev - er, nev - er bow we down to the rude stock or sculp - - tur'd

75

stone. But ev - er wor - - ship Is - - rael's

stone. But ev - er wor - - ship Is - - rael's

stone. But ev - er wor - - ship Is - - rael's

78

God, ev - - er o - be - dient to His aw - ful nod.

God, ev - - er o - be - dient to His aw - ful nod.

God, ev - - er o - be - dient to His aw - ful nod.

82

[segue]

162

164

170

END OF PART TWO

PART THREE

No. 48

Air FATHER OF HEAV'N

Israelitish Priest

the—Feast of—Lights, the—Feast of—Lights, to sol-emn-ize———— the

Feast of Lights, While we pre-pare with ho - - ly—rites, to

sol-emn-ize——————— the Feast of Lights.

And thus our grate - ful—hearts em -

Bars 31, 35, 48 and 63 have no figured bass in **A** and **B**. **W1** first suggested $^6_4$ $^5_3$ chords for beats 1 and 2 in these bars.
Bar 36, beat 1: **A** has 'fort'.
Bar 38, beat 3: **A** and **B** have $\curvearrowright$.

No. 49   Accompanied Recitative SEE, SEE YON FLAMES

Israelitish Man

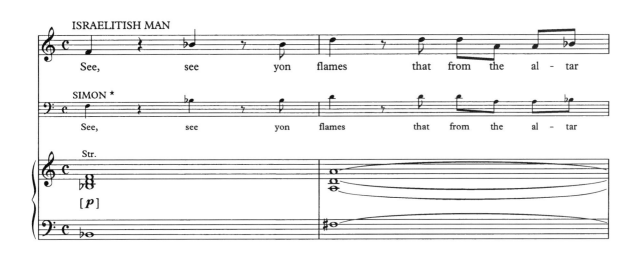

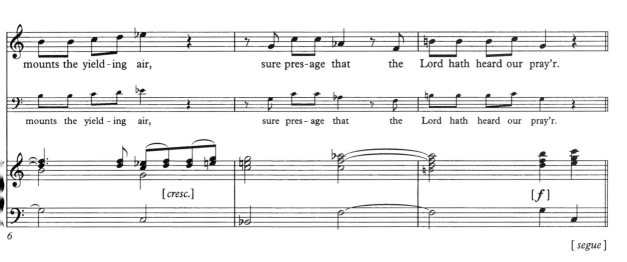

[segue]

---

* If the 1747 version is used this movement could be sung by the bass soloist. See Preface, p. xv.

No. 50　　　　　Recitative O GRANT IT, HEAV'N
Israelitish Woman

No. 51   Air   SO SHALL THE LUTE AND HARP AWAKE

Israelitish Woman

ISRAELITISH WOMAN

So shall the lute — and harp a-wake, and

spright-ly voice sweet des-cant run.   So

shall the lute— a -wake, so shall the harp— a - wake, so

[*p*]

15

shall the lute— and— harp a -wake, and spright-ly— voice sweet des - cant— run, and

17

spright - ly voice sweet des - - cant run, and spright - - - -

19

- - - - - - - - - ly voice sweet

22

des - cant run,_____ and spright - - - -

[*f*]

[*p*]

25

No. 52

Recitative FROM CAPHARSALAMA
Israelitish Messenger

ISRAELITISH MESSENGER

From Ca - phar - sa - la - ma, on ea - gle wings I

fly with ti - dings of im - pe - tuous joy. Came Ly - si - as, with his

host ar - ray'd in coat of mail; their mas - sy shields of gold and brass flash'd

light - ning o'er the fields, while the huge tow'r - back'd e - le - phants dis -

-play'd a hor - rid front. But Ju - das, un - dis - may'd,

met, fought, and van-quish'd all the rage-ful train.

Bars 12-14: solo part has both sets of notes in **B**.

No. 53   Air ALL HIS MERCIES

Israelitish Messenger

ISRAELITISH MESSENGER

All— his mer-cies—

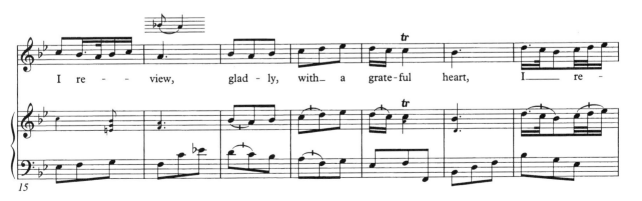

I re- view, glad-ly, with— a grate-ful heart, I— re-

Bar 17: marked 'v. pianiss' in *Athalia*.

he did once im - part, bless - ings, bless-ings
he did once im - part.

No. 54   Recitative YET MORE, NICANOR LIES

Israelitish Messenger

ISRAELITISH MESSENGER

Yet more, Ni - ca - nor lies with thou - sands slain; the

blas - phe-mous Ni - ca - nor, who de - fied the liv - ing God, and

in his wan-ton pride a pub-lic mo-nu-ment or-dain'd of vic-to-ries yet un-gain'd.

But lo! the con-que-ror comes, and on his spear, to dis - si -pate all fear, he

bears the vaun-ter's head and hand that threat-en'd de -so - la -tion to the land.

[segue]

ALTERNATIVE BASS VERSION ★

But lo! the con-que-ror comes, and on his spear, to dis - si-pate all fear, he

bears the vaun-ter's head and hand that threat-en'd de - so - la-tion to the land.

[segue]

★ See Preface, p. xv.

No. 55   Chorus SEE, THE CONQU'RING HERO COMES

Chorus of Youths

* The small notes are for rehearsal purposes only.

[segue]

194

Chorus of Virgins

[segue]

Chorus of Israelites

* See Preface, p. xiii.

** Handel wrote 'Drum ad libitum (i.e. extemporising), the second time warbling (i.e. playing drum rolls).'

he - ro comes, sound the trum - pets, beat the drums.

[segue]

No. 56

MARCH

* See Preface, p. xiii.

No. 57   Solo and Chorus   SING UNTO GOD

Chorus with A.T. soli

Sing un - to God, and high af - fec - tions raise, to

* See Preface, p. xiii.

57

60

63

No. 58   Recitative   SWEET FLOW THE STRAINS

Judas Maccabaeus

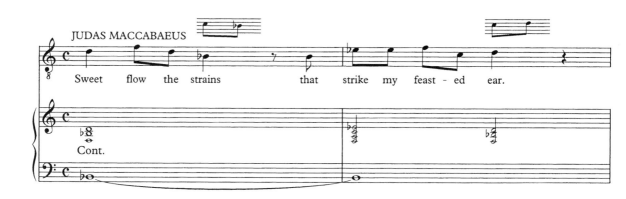

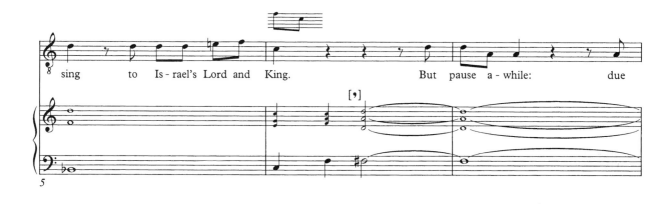

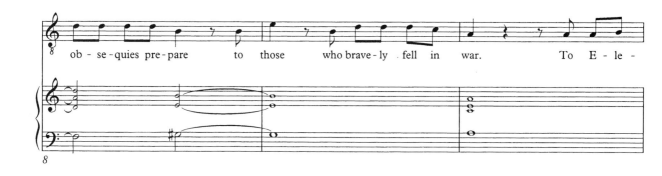

-a - zar spe - cial tri - bute pay. Through slaugh - ter'd

troops he cut his way to the dis - tin - guish'd e - le - phant, and, 'whelm'd be -

-neath the stab - bed mon - ster, tri - umph'd in a glo - rious death.

No. 59 Air WITH HONOUR LET DESERT BE CROWN'D

Judas Maccabaeus

Andante larghetto

* See Preface, p. xiii.

JUDAS MACCABAEUS

honour let desert be crown'd, the trumpet ne'er in vain shall sound, the

trumpet ne'er in vain shall sound.

But all at-ten-tive to a-larms, but

all at-ten-tive to a-larms the

will-ing na-tions fly to arms, to arms, to arms, and

con - quer-ing, or con-quer'd, claim,_____ and claim the prize of

hap - - -py earth, or far more_ hap-py_ skies, and

claim_____ the prize of hap - - -py earth, or far more hap - - py

skies.

No. 60   Recitative PEACE TO MY COUNTRYMEN

Eupolemus

No. 61   Chorus TO OUR GREAT GOD

Chorus

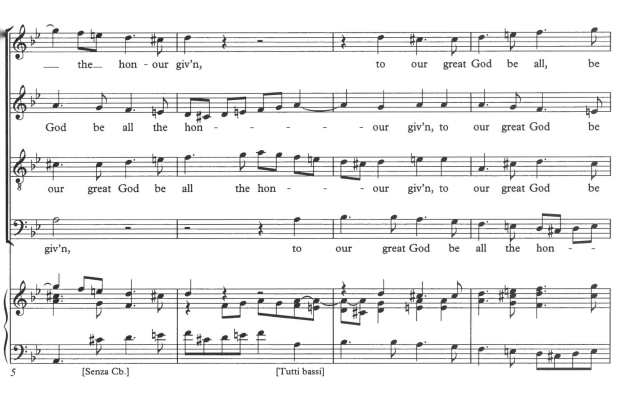

* See Preface, p. xiii.

Bar 1, bass stave: the two crotchet rests are editorial.

No. 62   Recitative AGAIN TO EARTH LET GRATITUDE DESCEND

Israelitish Woman

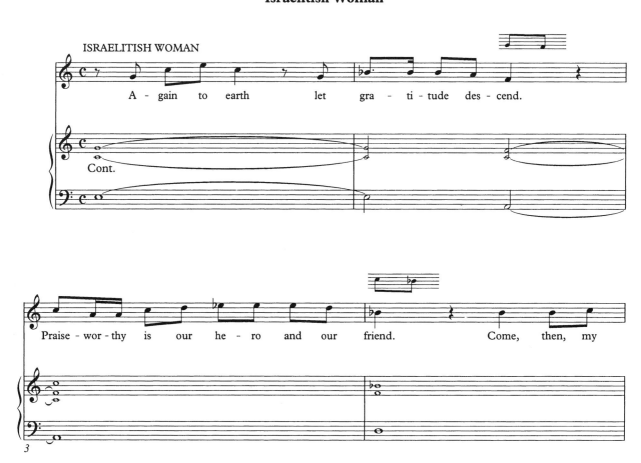

No. 63   Duet O LOVELY PEACE

Israelitish Woman, Israelitish Man

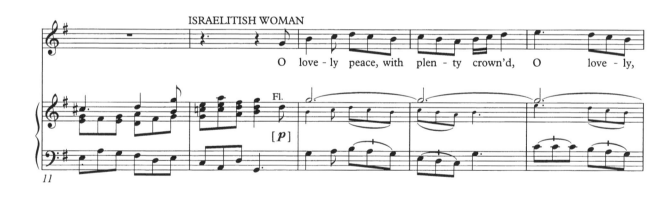

O love - ly peace, with plen - ty crown'd, O love - ly,

love - ly peace, come, spread thy__ bless - ings, thy__ bless - ings all__ a-round.

ISRAELITISH MAN

O

Bars 37-44: a cut was made in **B**. Since **W1** did not observe this, it is likely that it was made after 1747.
* Omit this note if the cut is made.

No. 64   Air and Chorus   REJOICE, O JUDAH. HALLELUJAH, AMEN

Simon, Chorus

-joice,_____ with Che - ru -bin and Se - ra-phin, har -

-mo - - - nious join in songs di -

-vine, with Che - ru -bin and Se - ra-phin, har - mo - - nious, har-

-mo - nious join.

Bar 47: no tempo marking was written here in **A** and **B**. In later printed editions 'Allegro' was added.

230

END OF THE ORATORIO

APPENDIX ONE
Variant movements for the 1750 revivals

No. 24b   Recitative O JUDAS, MAY THY JUST PURSUITS

Israelitish Man

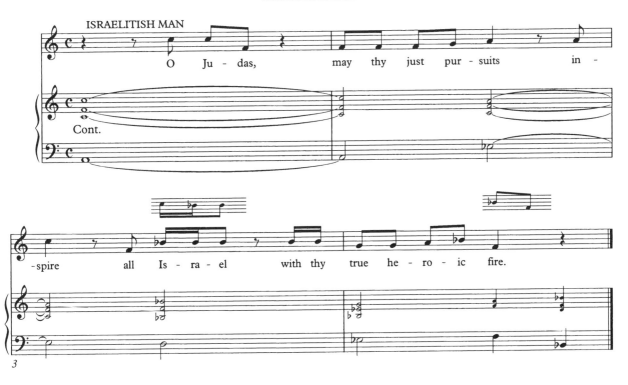

No. 25b   Air ENDLESS FAME

Israelitish Man

Bar 8, beat 2: the alternative rhythm above the stave appears in later printed editions of *Esther*.

234

thy faith-ful care, glo-ry bright-er than the

morn-ing shall re-ward___ thy faith - - ful care,___

___ shall re-ward___ thy faith - ful care.

No. 63b   Air O LOVELY PEACE

Israelitish Woman

thy___ bless - ings all___ a - round.

Tutti

[mf]

O love - ly, love - ly peace,___ come, spread___

Fl.

[p]

thy___ bless - ings, spread thy bless - ings all___ a - round, spread thy bless - ings

Tutti

[mf]

all___ a - round.

Let

[p]

flee - cy flocks the hills___ a - dorn, and val - leys smile with wa - vy corn.

Tutti

[mf]

239

val - leys smile with wa - vy corn, and val - leys smile with wa - vy corn, and

65

smile with wa - vy corn.

Tutti

[mf]

70

FINE

75

Let the shrill trum - pet cease, let the shrill trum - pet cease, nor

[p]

Str.

80

o - ther sound, but na - ture's song - - sters

Str.

pp

Vla.

84

[Tutti bassi]

wake the cheer - ful morn, nor o - - ther sound, but

na - ture's song - sters wake_____ the cheer - - - ful morn, nor

o - ther sound,___ but na - ture's song - sters wake the cheer - ful morn,

but na - ture's song - - - sters

wake, wake, wake_____ the cheer - ful morn.

APPENDIX TWO
Additional items for the original version of 1 April 1747

No. 6b Recitative NOT VAIN IS ALL THIS STORM OF GRIEF

Simon

Not vain is all this storm of grief, to vent our sor-rows gives re-lief.

Wretch-ed in-deed! But let not Ju-dah's race their ru-in with des-pond-ing arms em-

brace. Dis-tract-ful doubt and des-pe-ra-tion ill be-come the cho-sen Na-tion,

Cho-sen by the great I AM, the Lord of Hosts, who, still the

same, we trust will give at-ten-tive ear to the sin-ce-ri-ty of pray'r.

No. 16b   Recitative O JUDAS, MAY THESE NOBLE VIEWS INSPIRE

Israelitish Man

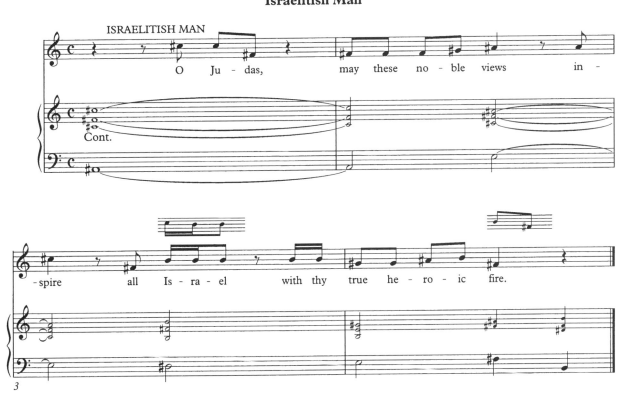

No. 52b   Recitative FROM CAPHARSALAMA

Israelitish Messenger

host ar-ray'd in coat of mail; their mas-sy shields of gold and brass flash'd

light-ning o'er the fields, while the huge tow'r-back'd e-le-phants dis-

-play'd a hor-rid front. But Ju-das, un-dis-may'd,

met, fought, and van-quish'd all the rage-ful train.

[*segue*]

No. 54b Recitative YET MORE, NICANOR LIES

Israelitish Messenger

APPENDIX THREE
Additional items for the 1758-9 version

No. 25c   Air   FAR BRIGHTER THAN THE MORNING

Israelitish Man

* The editorially suggested interpretation of ⊓ and ⌐· , as shown above in bars 1-9, applies throughout, except in bars 69-71, 85-87, 109, 115-116, 118, 120, 122, 126, 131 and 137-141.

* See footnote, p. 246

re - ward___ thy care,

[f]

+ Obs.

+ Bsn.

77

let fame re - ward thy care,   let fame re - ward thy care,

+ Hns.

81

Adagio   [*tr*]   **[a tempo]**

let fame re - ward___ thy care.

Adagio   **[a tempo]**
Tutti

[*p*]   [*f*]

85   Senza Bsn.

90

94

* See footnote, p. 246

* See footnote, p. 246

252

* See footnote, p. 246

No. 30b   Duet and Chorus SION NOW HER HEAD SHALL RAISE

Israelitish Woman, Israelitish Man, Chorus

No. 37b   Recitative **SWEET ARE THY WORDS**

Israelitish Man

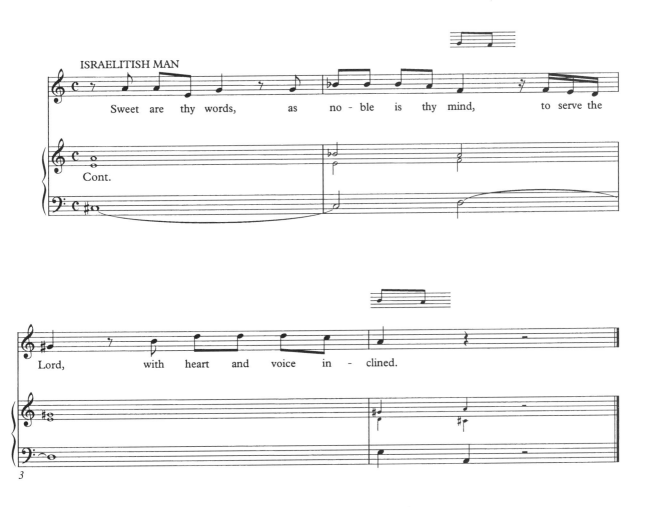

ISRAELITISH MAN

Sweet are thy words, as no - ble is thy mind, to serve the

Cont.

Lord, with heart and voice in - clined.

No. 37c   Air GREAT IN WISDOM

Israelitish Man

Obs., Vlns., Vla.

[Tutti bassi]

No. 46b   Air WISE MEN, FLATT'RING, MAY DECEIVE US

Israelitish Woman

Larghetto

[*f*] Fls., Obs., Bsns., Hns., Str.

p Senza Hns.

Soli Vc.*

* marked 'violone: soli' in **B** .

Bars 27-28 (and subsequently): 'deceive us' as in **B** and **L5**; 'deceive you' in **W2** and **J**.

274

No. 54c   Recitative YET MORE, NICANOR LIES

Israelitish Messenger

blas-phe-mous Ni - ca - nor, who de - fied the liv - ing God, and

in his wan-ton pride a pub-lic mo-nu-ment or-dain'd of vic-to-ries yet un-gain'd.

But lo! the con-que-ror comes, and on his spear, to dis - si - pate all fear, he

bears the vaun-ter's head and hand that threat-en'd de - so - la - tion to the land.

[segue]

The New Novello Choral Edition

For 150 years Novello vocal scores have made a unique contribution to British choral singing, providing a mixture of accuracy, clarity and competitive pricing that has been a benchmark for others to emulate.

In recent years, however, ever-improving standards of musical scholarship and music engraving have led Novello to launch a series of completely new editions of the most popular choral works that will continue to set the standard for decades to come.

- **Prepared by respected scholars to the highest editorial standards.**

- **Full introductions in several languages give details of the historical background to the work and the editorial issues involved.**

- **Completely re-engraved music pages using the most sophisticated setting systems.**

- **Large page-size for more generous spacing, yet retaining the layout of Novello's previous edition for ease of use in rehearsal, when both are often in use.**

All maintaining the Novello tradition of unbeatable value for money!

Currently available in the series:

Bach	*St Matthew Passion* ed. Neil Jenkins
Bach	*St John Passion* ed. Neil Jenkins
Handel	*Belshazzar* ed. Donald Burrows
Handel	*Judas Maccabaeus* ed. Merlin Channon
Handel	*Messiah* ed. Watkins Shaw
Haydn	*The Creation* (*Die Schöpfung*) ed. Michael Pilkington
Maunder	*Olivet to Calvary* rev. Michael Pilkington
Mendelssohn	*Elijah* ed. Michael Pilkington
Mozart	*Requiem* ed. Duncan Druce (also including Druce's own completion)
Rossini	*Petite Messe Solennelle* (separate chorus part also available)
Stainer	*Crucifixion* rev. Michael Pilkington
Verdi	*Requiem* ed. Michael Pilkington

The Handel Works also form part of the ongoing *Novello Handel Edition*